Downsizing Your Life: Minimalism for Real People

B. Vincent

Published by RWG Publishing, 2024.

While every precaution has been taken in the preparation of this book, the publisher assumes no responsibility for errors or omissions, or for damages resulting from the use of the information contained herein.

DOWNSIZING YOUR LIFE: MINIMALISM FOR REAL PEOPLE

First edition. June 20, 2024.

Copyright © 2024 B. Vincent.

Written by B. Vincent.

Table of Contents

Introduction 1
Part I: Understanding Minimalism 2
Part II: Benefits of Minimalism 4
Part III: Getting Started with Downsizing 6
Part IV: Practical Steps to Downsize 8
Part V: Embracing a Minimalist Lifestyle 10
Part VI: Overcoming Challenges 13
Part VII: Minimalism in Different Areas of Life 16
Part VIII: Maintaining Your Minimalist Lifestyle 18
Conclusion 21

Introduction

If you've done any research on this topic, you've probably run across one of the many 'life editing' blogs that are out there. Some are great resources, and have truly helpful advice on purging and paring back our lives. Others seem as though their standards are high enough to set out multiple place settings for company, but they die if you even look at them funny, which isn't real life at all for most of us. I want to show you a different side to editing your life. You can pare back your belongings and commitments to reasonable limits, and make the lifestyle work for you. You can get happy and comfortable with what you have, and what you don't. You can get ready to live the life you always meant to live, not the one that was forced on you by a mountain of credit card debt and the pressure to get and do as much as possible.

When you hear the term 'minimalism', what comes to mind? For many people, minimalism conjures images of stark white walls and furniture, spaces devoid of all but the most basic furnishings, and a life that centers around a simple set of philosophies and ideals. But minimalism doesn't have to mean empty. It's really about putting the best and most important things in the center of your life, while getting rid of the less important things that usually crowd our days. This book presents a real-world look at how living a simpler lifestyle can benefit you. It's full of ways to pare down the amount of stuff we have in our lives and to experience life to the fullest, without being so darned stressed and over-committed all the time. It can help you make that shift from having it all to having the best.

Part I: Understanding Minimalism

In this chapter, I've spent time developing the PowerPoint presentation, handouts, and training exercises that are used in conjunction with this informal discussion. All of these items are available through the Internet or at any Border's Book Store. To best understand how minimalism can be used to help downsize life, we need to understand what minimalism is. The obvious starting place is with a definition of minimalism. We have already read or heard how Webster's defines minimalism, now it's time to see how industry defines minimalism. Let's start with UseNet and look at the definitions of minimalism that developers are using.

Before we can explore ways to downsize, we need to have some understanding of how we got to the point where downsizing becomes desirable. To best accomplish this, I present a four-part definition of minimalism. The definition I've chosen to use comes from people, literary sources, and my own personal experiences as a manager and trainer. Most individuals and publications that refer to minimalism are consistent with this definition. Minimalism can be all or some of the following: a design principle that emphasizes the importance of doing only that which supports the business objective; a style of writing that allows very little, if any, unnecessary information; a business practice that seems; a state of ingrained response by the developer and the sponsor of a product. It is my premise that for us to comfortably downsize our lives, we first must understand minimalism and what, if any, potential it has for impacting our lives.

2.1. Chapter 1: What is Minimalism?

Minimalism is actually a delicate blend of both family and whitespace, so designed to transparently streamline the superfluous, make your individual designs the real star of your life's stage, and immediately pathway your incoming yearnings toward what's excitingly new, highly personal, and exclusively enriching. The minimalist approach accentuates the constantly vibrant posh of your contemporary evidence by insistently urging you to consolidate your skill pool until only the most perfectly creative surroundings remain; by ensuring your physical greatly admired presentation - by simply painting your world one or two tones brighter than your next caliber architect defines.

When urban condominiums leave your stagnant fantasies completely drained but rich, that's minimalism. When you decide that your car needs a quieter, less frenzied roar, and your four-bedroom asset castle doesn't make you happier anymore, well, that's minimalism. The minimal life doesn't mean emptying your closets, purging museum-quality collections, or denying your buried urges to savor the occasional quiet luxury of highly regarded treasures; it doesn't automatically translate to dropping out or adopting a spartan lifestyle.

Minimalism is one of those carefully selected, well-organized words that seems to have a striped shirt and tie personality. When most of us hear the word, we usually think of off-white walls, stark furnishings, and loosely scattered Japanese motifs. We might even think about creating new images on our computers, stacking bricks to form aqua-velvet patterns, or broad landscapes dusted with carefree Utopias. However, minimalism is actually an endearing lifestyle concept that deals with the great, liberating truth about your new beginning: Saying less will ultimately bring you infinitely more.

2.2. Chapter 2: Brief History of Minimalism

Historically speaking, minimalism is more than just an architectural style distilled from European Modernism. In the late sixties, it was an extensive and highly influential radical avant-garde, with emancipation and spiritual liberation as its main ideological thrust. In the sixties, Minimalist painting and sculptural style were largely developed by American artists, and it is important to realize that their American artistic tradition, and not a European one, is still crucial to the critical and ideological implications of the work modern minimalist enthusiasts graphically display in their magazines.

Minimalism, as a lifestyle, is on the rise. As if to forestall any suspicious whisperings about its ideological banality, current minimalist proponents mention in a full-page spree how minimalism has been around for centuries in ancient cultures. And how the architects of modernity, like Louis Sullivan and Mies van der Rohe, are praiseworthy minimalist clue-bearers. But then what is so modern about minimalism today, you really have to wonder.

Part II: Benefits of Minimalism

We feel better about our lives when there's less. Do you stay up at night pondering the clutter in your life? Doesn't it sound more comforting to have less to care about and fewer things to organize and clean? With less to distract us, we can pour ourselves into things we are truly passionate about. We can explore new things that we didn't have time for when we had too much stuff.

Living a minimalist life frees us. Minimalist living helps us clear our physical space by ridding ourselves of excess "stuff" and the emotional baggage that comes with it. Having too much material clutter inhibits us not only in our ability to clean our homes but also in our capacity to think and function effectively. This often creates frustration and dissatisfaction. Simplicity, in direct contrast, brings us a sense of calm and ultimately more joy.

3.1. Chapter 3: Physical Benefits

Not only does uncluttering make for a more efficient use of space, free mental space and reduce stress, it also saves you time in cleaning your things, daily searches for the missing ones, and opening spaces. A clear empty space does wonders for your outlook and often helps you make decisions with more ease. Managing your things and storage units takes time and skill; time that you could be devoting to your family. The modern house has invented the mudroom again to solve all its storage concerns but this outward symbol of our throwaway society can far more simply be removed if everything we purchased was neither superfluous nor surplus to our needs.

One of the greatest physical benefits of minimalism is lessening the storage issues that plague so many people in affluent societies. We are a society of store-aholics. We have meanwhile graduated from the land of yards and large spacious homes to the land of duplexes and apartment complexes that are supposed to afford us much greater leisure time. Far from it. The incredibly fast growth in property rental and warehouse storage services is reflective of the hidden cost of first world living. The value of investments in storage units moved from 8 billion in 1995 to well over 22 billion by 2009. We are currently spending 154 billion entirely on our desire to consume, and then buy more space to consume more so we can find the time to be able to quit working so hard to earn enough money to keep buying more stuff that doesn't really make us happy.

3.2. Chapter 4: Mental and Emotional Benefits

Mental and Emotional Benefits: There will be many mental and emotional benefits from owning fewer things. It is impossible to discuss them all due to the varying degrees of effects owning way more than each person needs has had on our lives. But here are some of the possible direct and immediate positive effects of owning fewer things. Money will have to be earned and, in turn, has to be spent. You are not owned by your things, implying less worry. Time needs to be spent doing the things you enjoy instead of managing your things. Family can become part of your lives—or move closer to where they currently should be. It is not instant, but minimalism can help change so many negative thoughts and emotions to happy and pleasant ones.

This is the section of the book called "Downsizing Your Life: Minimalism for Real People" that refers to the mental and emotional benefits of being a minimalist. This section of text presents possible direct and immediate positive mental and emotional effects from owning fewer things. It offers an explanation and reasoning behind each. The author challenges readers to break the ties society has placed on them.

Part III: Getting Started with Downsizing

This is just the beginning, and I hope you're ready to keep digging deeper because I can't possibly answer everything in one book or even in one chapter. There are so many areas in life that can be downsized. Each thing doesn't have to be categorized as Bill's, Sally Sue's, etc. Have groupings like "To Do," "Donate," "Action Needed," etc. Buy rubber bins (non-see through) that are ecofriendly. They could be recycled and are usually made out of 100% percent post-consumer recycled cardboard. Use a permanent marker to label each box with category labels like "Keep," "Throw," "Donate," "Sell" and use a different color of a permanent marker to write each person's name on their boxes.

It's great talking about something, but until you can apply the principles to your everyday life, it's all just talk. And you're ready to get started, right? Well, there's something I must tell you: this is work. It takes time and patience. But if you get a system down, it'll become a part of your life. Eventually it will become second nature and everything you bring in will be thought through and scrutinized. Your life will be clutter-free and you won't believe the time, money, energy and headaches this has saved you.

4.1. Chapter 5: Assessing Your Current Situation

Ask yourself questions like these: - Are you happy with your lifestyle, or does your life stress you out? Does your life overwhelm you with busyness, complexity, or clutter? - Does your life's clutter or busyness give you comfort, security, a sense of identity, happiness, status, or meaning, or do they block you or stress you out? - What drives you to possess, do, be, or want particular things? What would you have left, and who would you be without them? What if you stopped wanting all this stuff? Why haven't you yet? - How do you spend your time on an average day? What's the most satisfying thing you do during a typical day or week? What do you enjoy most outside of work? How or when does your life's clutter or busyness block the things you love? Why haven't you decluttered? - What are your goals, dreams, and ideals? What are your beliefs and meanings? What's important and satisfying in life? Why haven't you achieved them, taken them seriously, or followed your dreams? What's stopping you? What are your biggest obstacles or roadblocks? - How do you measure success or self-worth? How do you think others perceive you? How do you want others to see you?

This is one of the most difficult parts of downsizing your life: to finally assess where you are, how you got there, and where you want to go. These are big questions - don't rush the answers, but at the same time, don't procrastinate, live in denial, over-analyze, obsess, or become paralyzed with fear or lack of time or knowledge. They're just questions, and you're strong and capable enough to find the answers.

4.2. Chapter 6: Setting Goals for Downsizing

It's important to be clear what your goals are. When I started off, I wrote myself a list of goals so that I would remember why I was doing this on days when the effort to downsize seemed overwhelming. My goals were to have a neat, organized and clean house; to simplify everything; to create a warm, welcoming, and comfortable living environment without a lot of stuff to maintain; to establish healthy living habits in respect to exercise, eating, and cooking, and to enjoy the cooking process; and, to develop outdoor and social interests that don't involve buying unnecessary stuff or eating hours away. I wanted my new way of life to be about quality, not quantity of goods and activities. The day when I wrote those goals was the day I went into mad decluttering mode.

You won't get where you are going if you don't know where you are trying to go. Goals for simplifying your life are crucial. You need to define what you want to achieve, and then break these goals down into manageable steps. When you are downsizing your life, the best place to start is by setting manageable goals. Don't tell yourself you have to cook all your meals from scratch starting tomorrow if you usually eat takeout and microwave meals. Instead, tell yourself you will cook five meals from scratch this month, and maybe up that to seven next month. Setting your sights too short is the quickest way to quit.

Part IV: Practical Steps to Downsize

Nonetheless, let me offer a practical plan to work through your downsizing task. Earlier I promised that by the end of this section, you would lose 200 pounds. I have every intention of keeping that promise. Granted, the weight loss is met only metaphorically, but the benefits of this weight loss will be very real, indeed. At the end of this process, you will have all the tools, techniques, and encouragement needed to manage any downsizing task. Because I started small and doubled the weights only a few times, every pound of weight lost seems to be experienced as a minor triumph. Do the same thing, and no task in your downsizing process should ever appear to be outrageously huge. Each one should be just big enough—no larger and certainly not smaller.

Life is not simplistic, so a simplistic answer to the question seems unlikely to solve our downsizing issues. As I said in the introduction, I am a very practical person. That is why I did not offer impractical suggestions along with empty promises. "Throw it out" is advice almost guaranteed to be overlooked. Dirt simple or not, this task is something only you can do in your way. Your effort counts.

5.1. Chapter 7: Decluttering Your Home

Organize on purpose. Get everything in one place from both living spaces, and decide exactly what it is that you need. Then organize it and get rid of the rest. I'm not saying do it on the same day, but do it soon. One of these days is enough, because you say when that special day is going to be. Just be serious before you start, and organize. Then divide up your stuff and do it in sections. Depending on how much you have and what style of organizer you are, you could start at the beginning of a week, or do it on weekends. I'm not a professional organizer and can't come to your home to raid through your stuff, so it's your job to get organized and get started. In order to make everything you pick as organized as it can be, I'm going to walk you through some ideas from every expert that I'm allowed to.

Wouldn't it be nice to have a clutter-free home? Take a look at the rooms you use the most. Maybe you have a garage you can't park your car in because it's full of stuff, a basement where you're afraid to go because you could never find anything down there, even though you know it's exactly what you have to have somewhere in your stash of stuff. Aren't you curious what you're storing down there? What's so important it's worth having to live with all the rest of the junk that you hate anyway? Have you ever thought that the reason you can't find stuff is because you have so much?

5.2. Chapter 8: Managing Digital Clutter

If you're not the slightest bit interested in clearing out your digital debris or in gaining some clutter-busting checklists for maintaining your sacred personal digital space, I give you permission to bail on reading the rest of this chapter right now. If, however, you feel like your digital life could use a little organizing and streamlining, read on. There is such a complex set of virtual gadgets and systems that people need help with, that the digital clutter choices seem impossible to deal with. You need only think of digital clutter as a mirror image of the physical world and start doing some sorting.

After you're all decluttered in the physical world, the next and perhaps final frontier is cleaning up your digital environment. I know sometimes you have to create and save things in digital space that wouldn't be considered important or beautiful enough to save in the physical world. I realize that if you write a report for work, you aren't likely to want to file that away in a special drawer indefinitely. Anyone who creates digital things to share with others will need to organize and store them in some manner.

Part V: Embracing a Minimalist Lifestyle

360. With fewer goods around, many people will redistribute work giving a new sense of significance to the emptiness of time. Giving model-building citizens new opportunities will create a slower, more varied way of life. With greater abundance, we will be able to conserve the land, clean the air, and grow the food that we need in ways that use resources wisely and meet our grandest, most humane ideals. The very institutions and forces that might seem to make change difficult - schools, churches, commerce, and community - become our means of signaling what is most valuable in life. By redistributing work and decreasing the amount of goods that we buy, we are able to ask for the real necessities of life.

359. What you are doing at the present time is what is most important. Through diminishing the goods produced by the multinational companies, you can help them focus on creating the goods that you really need. As we buy fewer clothes, cars, and houses with the Equal Opportunity logo, we are able to dictate what we want produced and how we want it distributed. When this happens, the multinational companies start a new flow of resources and change their direction accordingly. Instead of maintaining surplus resources to handle peak periods, production is reduced and streamlined to meet projected needs.

358. Changing from a fast-paced, materialistic lifestyle to a streamlined, minimalist lifestyle requires that you change in an area where change is most difficult, an area that has the most influence. Only when you begin to choose the messages you let inside yourself will life have the meaning that you want it to have.

357. The messages that influence our buying habits make the biggest impact. For instance, when you are told that what you wear indicates your intelligence, speech, and competence, you are being asked to buy something in order to gain something. The multibillion-dollar cosmetic and fashion industries depend on their ability to create, enhance, and play upon the need for expression and self-identity.

6.1. Chapter 9: Mindful Consumption

Doesn't that sound exhausting? I once had a similar conversation with a friend of mine who is extremely proud of her frequent miles and her multiple credit cards. I asked her, "Is all this worth it?" and she looked at me as if the realization that life could be different had never actually occurred to her. "No," she said. "It's not. But I don't know what else to do. What would I do otherwise? What would I do?" It's this "fear of missing out" that keeps the economy churning, fads changing, and businesses advertising. Earning money, buying whatever your culture or subculture tells you that you "need," and consuming the latest and greatest, often just to prove that you can, is happening in our lives. Going against this requires mindfulness. It requires considering that the price of those shoes is more than just the dollar amount. It requires considering the time spent with your children at a stressful job versus, say, not spending money, having less stress, and therefore not needing that same as high salary - therefore allowing yourself to potentially work less.

"I was $20,000 in credit card debt with seven credit cards all maxed out at the same time," wrote my friend Lorilee Lippincott. "We bought top-of-the-line groceries even though they had no place to go and rotted in our refrigerator. The toys and plastic gadgets we acquired left our house cluttered. Our budgets suffered because of our ridiculous amount of stuff. We worked contracts just to pay off our debts. Every weekend [my husband], David, and I were busy with church activities. We filled weekends with friends, meetings, volunteering, dinner parties, and for me at the time, attending every baby or bridal shower I was invited to. Friends, events, and our stuff were still unable to fill the holes in our lives. We no longer let time or money work for us; we lived for spending it."

6.2. Chapter 10: Simplifying Your Finances

Many downsizers decide that simplification of their finances is a natural component of the downsizing process. Often, they find that craving less stuff and activity fits hand and pocketbook by ball game with the lessons and shortcuts they have learned about money. By focusing on only that which matters, they find that it is relatively easy to redirect their cash and their wisdom and experience in making financial decisions that matter. The strategies they use for accomplishing their chosen mission by being largely and wisely frugal, living debt-free, investing simply, and spending less time worrying about financial goals and allowing more time to experience rewards is the focus of this chapter. In the overspending and fast-lane life that so many of us lead, the concept of living within our means is not followed or even considered. Contrary to current beliefs, improved housing and other amenities don't necessarily make us happy. The rewards and satisfactions of life that can be achieved through the simple statement of "I have all I need and enough savings to let problems pass me by" are countered by few others.

Despite the financial worries that plague many Americans, it is the rare person who has only one goal when it comes to the accumulation and distribution of wealth. Your goals vary from buying a home and saving for your child's education to funding your retirement and taking that long trip around the world. Chapter 10 offers the opportunity to profit from living minimally by simplifying what is often complicated and financially profitable but time-consuming and nerve-fraying. You will manage money with less stress and still reach a satisfying chugging sound in your bank account and your financial engines. If you are part of a one-income or high-income couple, you may decide to downshift to a smaller salary and shift your lives into a lower gear. You may cut back to a lesser career where your job can provide benefits beyond money, such as chances to socialize, enjoy your friends, and experience a slower pace.

Part VI: Overcoming Challenges

When you replace a large dream with a smaller one, there are going to be a lot of people who cannot understand your dreams. With family and friends, explain yourself as much as you can, as clearly as you can, and in as much detail as you can. Most importantly, let your kids know why you are using less if they are aware of all the stuff they are losing. In our consumer culture, you will be labeled eccentric, odd, cheap, self-righteous, or anti-American if you choose not to keep up with the majority of the other consumers. These terms are choices other people might use to make themselves feel better about their lifestyle choices. They have nothing to do with you or the way you live. In some cases, you may be challenged by the things being said. If not, they will at least give you a clearer understanding of one of the challenges you face.

It is not easy to do something different. In our culture, experiences are directly associated with having stuff. We have to change that belief to truly embrace a minimalist lifestyle. Once you tell your friends that you are downsizing, you might be surprised to find that they are willing to help you because they are interested in what you are doing. It's also important to surround yourself with a certain level of support - if possible. Sharing information and enthusiasm about your downsizing endeavors can maximize your success rate.

7.1. Chapter 11: Dealing with Sentimental Items

But a time comes when sentimental items become the anchors and ballast in the ship of our lives. They drag us down and pull us back into our past when we need to be living for today. We consistently see people who, while they're out of storage room for their own things, purchase new homes (or even rent new storage space) specifically to hold all their "priceless" items. It seems that the more sentimental items a person keeps, the less sentimental value they all have. Instead of providing comfort, they seem to foster a low-level discontent in the house—there's just too much stuff. Too much maintenance. Too much emotional attachment. We know some people who have dozens of high school and college yearbooks, an extensive collection of other memorabilia, and lots of old clothing from their characters who often play dress-up. Their massive collections occupy two-thirds of the total storage space of their home. They've lived there for nearly ten years, and their eventual dream of renovating the master bathroom and turning it into a truly blissful in-house retreat was halted only because they didn't have anywhere to store all of their stuff during the remodel.

It's time to talk about the "S" word. No, not that one! We're talking about the dreaded and inevitable "Sentimental" items—those things that evoke emotions and memories unlike any others. Everyone has these items, ranging from the trivial (an old smoker's rack from college and expired pizza delivery menus) to the major (heirloom furniture and photos). Some of us even have saved nearly every souvenir from every vacation, every card from every event, and every trinket ever presented to us. Though we have little use or space for these items today, we cling to them with the unshakable belief that we absolutely cannot part with them. If we do, we fear intense regret over losing a priceless piece of our past and possibly disavowing those we love.

7.2. Chapter 12: Resisting the Urge to Re-Accumulate

The most difficult part of retaining your minimalist new life is having the ability to resist an overabundance of merchandise, marketing enablers, and personal purchase justifiers related to apparel, accessories, electronics, toys, collectibles, pet items, and games. Too often, people who recognize an issue with overabundance and begin a minimalist way of life, either moving or not, eventually resume past habits and are unable to cope with the many consumerism options that are no longer under lock and key. Items are needed. Preferences change, as well as sizes. If you have stopped using one item, plan for a decision on upgrading something else or the purchase of a new one. You should have within yourself requirements and guidelines if, in fact, that is really what you want or if that's just status quo belief. There are so many factors that will affect your decision. You didn't have to have that discussion when your space was already previously filled.

When post processed, we tend to believe that the habits we had in the pre-processed world can return and can be controlled. If we keep buying things because we believe we are once again disciplined consumers, we are very naive. Post-processed life will change your habits, permanently or temporarily. Move to a smaller place - no attic, no garage, no basement. Wouldn't it be easier to downsize and then give yourself a year to forever stop cold turkey the horizontal, unending buying odyssey? Well, yes, but you will probably lie to yourself since you are an optimist, but also because of post-processed belief. Surely you have learned your lesson and are ready for the old ways to return.

Part VII: Minimalism in Different Areas of Life

Making Time to Have a Life Outside of Work is necessary to live a balanced, satisfied life. Even the concept of Being a Nice Human—engaging in random acts of kindness as well as just always being there for family and friends—is a type of minimalism. We are keeping those things in our lives that are of the highest value to us and possible axes to everyone and everything else. Unlike the other areas of minimalism, Being a Nice Human is an area in which having more is less. If we are to have the time to spend with family and friends and to begin, maintain, or deepen our other interpersonal relationships, we have to give up other activities with a negative return on investment (with the exception being maintaining our own health and personal interests, which is separate).

Most people think of minimalism as decluttering a physical space. Lean Space and Lean Work are two areas you might already do at least some of if you have a Lean Home, but running that process in your life as a whole can be a bit of a new trend, at least in terms of naming and fashion. Extreme Hours is the area of minimalism of using our time efficiently. We all only have 24 hours in a day, but often our professional organizations have demands on a significant number of those hours to the detriment of our personal lives. Extreme Hours is the recognition that none of us like to spend much time working. If we could work much less or even not at a paid job at all with little-to-no impact on our quality of life, we would. Low Maintenance is what most of us think of when we think of minimalism: owning few things, getting rid of most possessions, and living in a beautifully and functionally bare space. It is the removal of most stuff from a part of our lives.

8.1. Chapter 13: Minimalist Wardrobe

Even men who wear suits and ties to work every day can get by with owning half of what is currently in their closets. A basic wardrobe would consist of: two suits (or three, depending on how often you think you need to wear one), ten dress shirts, two dressy sweaters, five pairs of conservative slacks, two pairs of casual pants, three dress-or-casual jackets, three belts, two ties, six pairs of dress socks, six pairs of casual socks, three white undershirts, and three pairs of business shoes or dressy casual shoes. If you are currently working in a position that requires you to wear a suit every day, you might feel more comfortable cutting back your wardrobe once you ease into your new decluttered lifestyle. In the first phase, simply replace the items you wear most often with higher-quality, classic styles. Later, when you're more comfortable having less to wear, you can pare down your remaining items to the numbers shown here.

8.1.1. The Men

Despite what you might believe, you don't actually need two outfits to wear every single day of the year. If you have a combination of those simple "basics," in mixed and matchable styles instead of the latest trends, laundering your clothing daily isn't quite such a necessity.

8.2. Chapter 14: Minimalist Travel

The interesting part to me though is how exhilarating it is to be on the road, carrying all of these material possessions. Because usually I have so few things and can fit them all in a small bag, I don't feel vulnerable, I feel empowered. No matter what happens, I can take care of it for myself. In our modern, marketing-driven world, all of our things are supposed to protect us. From discomfort, from boredom, from inactivity, from having to think at all while we entertain ourselves. These accumulated layers we think are standing between us and the harsh world are far more insidious than anything that could happen to us while on the road traveling. When you strip most of them away, you're free of them. The world can be however it's going to be, and you can accept it on its own terms. It's a paradox that only those who've experienced it can understand.

I'm an old hand at traveling around the world with a backpack. It started for me in my early twenties and has continued off and on through today. I relish the total feeling of freedom that comes from being able to carry everything you need to live your life on your back. No packing, no unpacking and repacking, nothing to check and it's not cumbersome. Once you're all packed, you're good to go. So, while I may travel heavy during my journey, my life is still pretty minimal on the road.

When you liberate yourself from your stuff, your stuff can be anywhere.

Part VIII: Maintaining Your Minimalist Lifestyle

It's fun for me to think about ways to keep things simple without feeling bored, let alone ready to chew my arm off in order to escape from the unfair, unreasonable restrictions that I've placed on myself. Maintaining your simple life, if you're in the right mental space, is a really fun part of the process. I've enjoyed putting this chapter together and hope that you enjoy reading it.

I know what you're thinking. "Haven't you taught me everything there is to know about caring for less? Why would maintaining a minimalist lifestyle require its own special chapter?" Well, you're right, I suppose. But I think it's worth discussing. After all, it's so easy to get caught up in the activity of decluttering that we don't spend much time thinking about what comes afterwards. Unfortunately, as we've heard so many times before, maintenance is critical. Without a good plan to maintain what we've accomplished, we'll inevitably find ourselves back in the old situation. But always remember, decluttering is never a one-time thing, but rather an ongoing process.

Chapter 33 - "Downsizing Is Not a One-Time Event" - Decluttering: An Ongoing Activity If You Want a Simple Life - Discuss Maintenance - The Fun Part: How to Keep It Simple Without Feeling Bored - The Fun Part: Growing - The Fun Part: Priorities - The Fun Part: Goals

9.1. Chapter 15: Creating Sustainable Habits

Wouldn't it be great if we could harness our natural love of habits to create the lifestyle we love practically overnight? Unfortunately, it isn't that easy. Not only do you have to sustain this habit over time, but you also have to make sure you're staying on the path while you're creating the habit. Creating habits is what you're doing while downsizing your life. You're breaking through your old habitual patterns by taking new, deliberate actions until the day arrives that you can perform them with hardly any thought or effort. In the process, you're creating good, new actions and brain patterns. You're creating a habit. Then, if you want to reach for a cookie and immediately discard it, then you start your process of breaking an old habit and creating a new one. For this book, since we're talking about minimalism, we're not only discussing creating habits but also how to start making them a part of your new and improved life.

No matter which habits you decide to embark on, habits don't get created overnight. As humans, we need repetition to drive a habit into our lives. The good news is that our brains are set up for that, as they put actions on autopilot so the brain can function on other, more complex tasks. Brains are wonderfully efficient at learning to execute all your habitual behaviors at the most convenient times. And this has distinct advantages. First, you have all that routine and regularity working for you. Second, once you've told your brain to take over, neurologists have found that the prefrontal cortex - located right behind your forehead - goes into a hibernation mode. This is the newest, most "me" part of your brain - responsible for most of your decision making. It's also the part of your brain that wears out as the day goes along. So when we let habits take over, the brain region that's taken the responsibility - the "habit center" - conserves energy.

Chapter 15: Creating Sustainable Habits

9.2. Chapter 16: Staying Motivated

When crowded with too much junk information, too many demands on our time, too much confusion about what's truly important, too many electrified adventure housekeeping robots, and too little leisure time, it's easy to forget why simplicity makes perfect sense. What are you fully, 100 percent, absolutely, down to your hard white peaceful core doing this journey toward a downsized life?

Your Greatest Intention

List those values that are challenged by your life now, that you've lost, that you'd like to enhance, or that you'd like to attain. What is important to me now? What do I desire? What needs do I wish to have met?

List Your Values

Both from our own experiences and feedback from readers, we know that staying motivated is the most difficult part of using voluntary simplicity to make positive changes in your life. Feeling wimpy? Or wondering if the heavy lift is worth it? You're not alone. But you can make it. It's okay to feel as uncertain as we often do.

How to Stay on Track

Downsizing is difficult, whether you're giving up favorite things, cutting back on hobbies, or making any other sacrifice. You have to really value the end result in order to stick with the plan. If you're downsizing your life, there are a number of things you might want more of in your life, including simplicity, happiness, control over time and space, freedom, peace of mind, balance, security, creativity, or financial independence. Increase your long-term focus and support this vision by building these personal rewards into the planning, decision making, and celebrating of your journey.

Conclusion

In a deeply strange way, minimalism has given me exactly that. It has simplified things. Has added clarity. It has decluttered my headspace. And in doing so, what is left is contentment; a quiet that I never knew before. And for that, I am immensely grateful. I'm not saying that my minimalism journey is at an end; it's a work in progress. My goal now is not to get rid of everything that I own but to keep only the things that give me sanity, joy, comfort, and peace. I love Keith's closing line in his book where he says, "Hold space for the things that matter." That's what I intend to do.

At first, my minimalist journey intimidated and overwhelmed me. What began as an exercise to downsize the mountain of belongings surrounding me quickly shifted into a complete audit of how I was living. The real epiphany was that almost everything beyond the essentials that I own is painful for me to own them and yet I still do. This includes things that are meant to improve my life in some way; things that I thought might be fun, entertaining, and worthwhile investments of my time and money. Things that are emotionally tied to a memory or a loved one. What I came to realize is that all of that represents debt. Not just in terms of time freely given, but a tax upon my energy, my focus, and my peace of mind. And nothing is more valuable to me than peace of mind.

Milton Keynes UK
Ingram Content Group UK Ltd.
UKHW040939081224
452111UK00011B/235